TOURIST RAILWAYS OF FRANCE

The sub-metre gauge lines

John Organ

Series editor Vic Mitchell

Front cover: Former Toury Sugar Refinery Decauville 0-6-0T no.5 and Borsig Feldbahn 0-8-0TT no.7 were viewed outside the CFCD workshop at Froissy, prior to hauling their respective trains in September 2015. (P.Dubocq / D.Blondin coll.)

Rear cover upper: The CF Forestier D'Abreschviller Heilbronn 0-4-4-0T Mallet was crossing the small bridge near the intermediate station at Rommelstein, when it was recorded during July 2007. (N.Moser)

Rear cover lower: One of the two Henschel Feldbahn 0-8-0Ts that operate on the CF des Combes was witnessed whilst climbing from Le Creusot at this fascinating system on 18th July 2007. (T.Kautzor)

Published April 2017

ISBN 978 1 910356 04 3

© Middleton Press, 2017

Production Editor Deborah Esher
Typesetting & design Cassandra Morgan
Cover design Matthew Esher

Published by
    Middleton Press
    Easebourne Lane
    Midhurst
    West Sussex
    GU29 9AZ
Tel: 01730 813169
Email: info@middletonpress.co.uk
www.middletonpress.co.uk

Printed and bound by CPI Group (UK) Ltd, Croydon, CR0 4YY

CONTENTS

1. CHEMIN de Fer TOURISTIQUE de PITHIVIERS
2. FROISSY – CAPPY – DOMPIERRE
   (Le P'tit Train de la Haute Somme)
3. CHEMIN de Fer FORESTIER D' ABRESCHVILLER
4. CHEMIN de Fer de la VALLÉE de L'OUCHE
5. CHEMIN de Fer TOURISTIQUE du TARN
6. THE "NEW" TOURIST RAILWAYS
   (Haute-Rhône, Chanteraines, Tacot des Lacs, Les Combes, Lac de Rillé.)

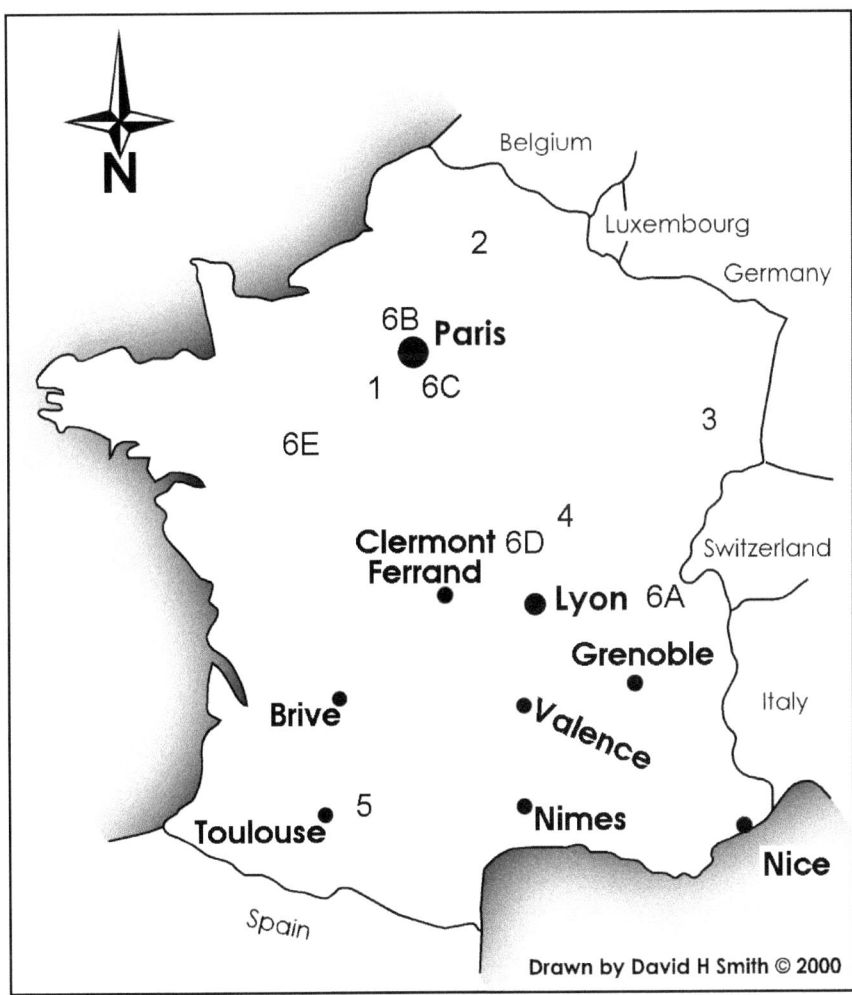

I. An outline map of France showing the location of the railways featured. The numbers relate to the section headings used in this publication. (D.H.Smith)

ABBREVIATIONS

ACFA	Association du Chemin de Fer Forestier d'Abreschviller
ACOVA	Association pour la Conservation Occitane de Véhicules Anciens
AMTP	Association du Musée des Transports de Pithiviers
APPEVA	Association Picarde pour la Préservation et l'Entretien des Véhicules Anciens
CFCD	Chemin de Fer Froissy-Cappy-Dompierre
CFTM	Chemin de Fer Touristique du Meyzieu (later changed to Montalieu)
CFTT	Chemin de Fer Touristique du Tarn
CFVO	Chemin de Fer de la Vallée de l'Ouche
FACS	Fédération des Amis des Chemins de Fer Secondaires
O & K	Orenstein & Koppel AG
SNCF	Société Nationale des Chemins de Fer Francais
TPT	Le Tramway Pithiviers à Toury

ACKNOWLEDGEMENTS

The compilation of this album would not have been possible without the invaluable assistance received from my many contacts in Britain, France and Switzerland. I therefore offer my sincere thanks to David Blondin (APPEVA), Bob Cable, Alain Elambert (AMTP), Philip Horton, David Huntbatch, Peter Johnson, Thomas Kautzor, Nicolas Moser (ACFA), Fabien Mottet, Philip Pacey, Brian Pearce, David Smith, James Waite, Chris Walker and Jeremy Wiseman. I must also thank Martyn Knight and Glynda Styles for checking the text and adding their suggestions.

INTRODUCTION

In addition to the many Metre Gauge systems throughout the country, as featured in our companion album *French Metre Gauge Survivors*, France also possessed a large number of railways of smaller gauges. These Petit lines were utilized for both passenger and industrial usage, although the latter were predominately more common. These were originally derived from the principles established by Paul Decauville (1846–1922) which involved lightweight railway infrastructure, often incorporating portable track sections, which were extensively employed in agricultural and industrial applications.

Following a successful 3km long demonstration line that served the Paris Exhibition of 1889, a number of 600mm gauge lines were constructed throughout France based on the formula of lightweight track and stock as used at Paris. The three notable systems that evolved at this time were the tramway at Royan, the extensive system at Calvados, both of which were principally passenger carrying lines, and the mainly agricultural network that linked the major sugar refineries at Pithiviers and Toury.

The Great War saw extensive use made of 600mm gauge supply lines built to Decauville principles by both sides of the conflict. Apart from one notable exception, which was adapted for industrial use after the war, these "trench railways" had a very short life. However they did provide much equipment, especially locomotives, which were given a new lease of life on many commercial lines that survived the war years.

This album will concentrate on the principal surviving historic lines from the late 19th century and early 20th century. Although only a few short sections of these have survived and have been adapted as tourist operations, including one that utilised a former standard gauge track bed, many more "new" systems have been created since 1962 on virgin sites. These have provided homes for numerous locomotives and items of rolling stock that would otherwise have become homeless and facing an uncertain future, following the closure of their former homes. Invariably the locomotives constructed by the Decauville factory are a predominant feature of these lines, whilst from the wartime period the German WWI Feldbahn machines have become an equally ubiquitous part of the French narrow gauge scene. Many of these were purchased in the immediate post war years, some of which were newly constructed and hardly used. By comparison, the locomotives of the Allied contribution to the war effort were mainly returned to British soil, although four American built machines remained in France and enjoyed an active life for many years.

1. CHEMIN de Fer TOURISTIQUE de PITHIVIERS

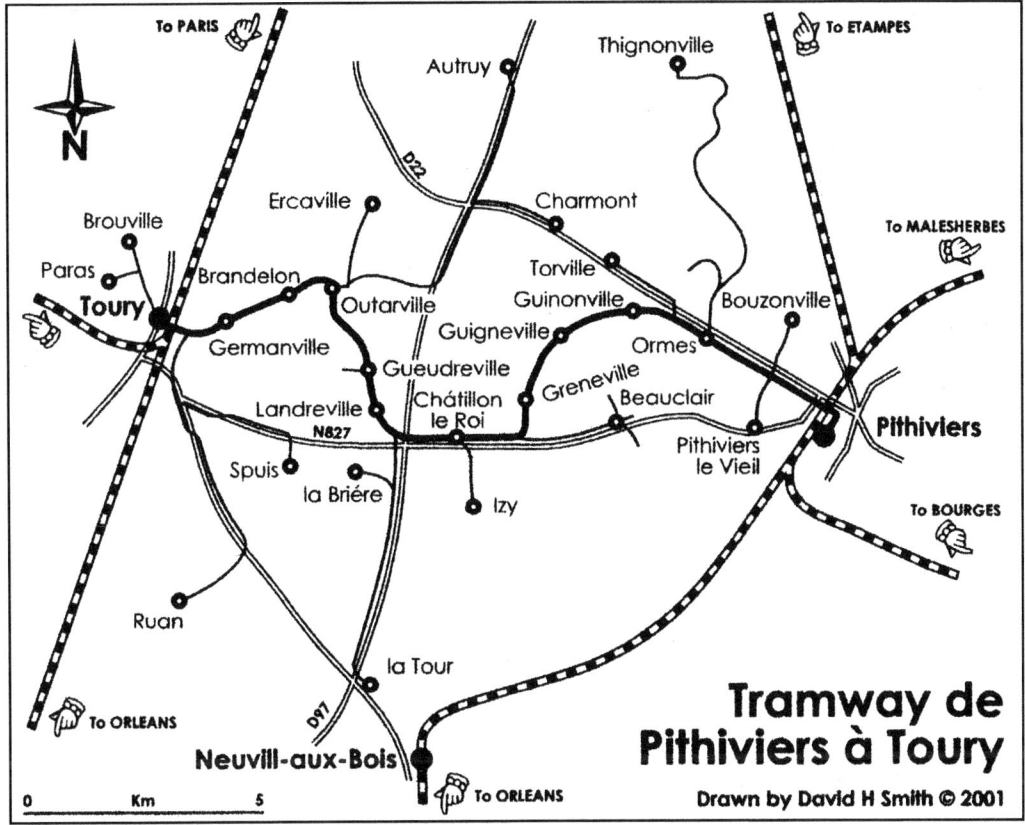

II. The full extent of the TPT system is shown in this map. The preserved section is confined to the eastern extremity of the former main line of the route. (D.H.Smith)

We begin our journey, exploring the surviving examples of the once extensive network of French minor railways, at the pioneer preserved line of any gauge throughout the country. Although schemes to save and acquire locomotives and rolling stock had begun on a limited scale as early as 1958, it was the closure of the Tramway de Pithiviers à Toury (TPT) in 1964 that saw the creation of a scheme to save part of this historic system in Loiret, 80km south-west of Paris.

The TPT was one of the first lines to be originally constructed and operated by Société Decauville, when it opened in 1892. The 31km long 600mm gauge line was conceived to link the towns of Pithiviers and Toury, both of which boasted extensive sugar refineries. The mainly roadside tramway was used extensively during the sugar beet harvesting period, whilst at other times it was used for the conveyance of general merchandise in addition to a limited passenger service. The Decauville principles of lightweight portable track were used to great effect during the harvesting months when many sidings sprouted from the "main line" in order to facilitate the gathering of crops, whilst as many as 15 locomotives would be active on one day.

During its 72 years existence, the TPT acquired a total of 35 locomotives of various sizes for use on its core business, whilst passenger services were mainly catered for by a quartet of small railcars, the first of which arrived in 1922. The steam locomotives ranged from small Decauville 0-4-0T and 0-6-0T machines plus equivalent types from other manufacturers, whilst the legacy of WWI provided an assortment of powerful engines from both sides of the conflict. The final additions to the stock arrived in 1945 with the acquisition of four new and unused Franco-Belge KDL type 0-8-0s which were among a large number built for the German war effort during WWII but never used. These were converted into 0-8-0T configuration at the extensive Pithiviers workshops following their arrival. One of the TPT former British War Department ALCO 2-6-2Ts has resided in Britain since 1967 and is now better known as the Ffestiniog Railway's "Mountaineer".

1.1   A classic view of the TPT operation was depicted as ALCO 2-6-2T no.3-20 hauled a load of sugar beet along the roadside tramway in 1963. (AMTP /J.F.Organ coll.)

1.2 Harvesting was in progress when sister ALCO no.3-23 was viewed as it joined a branch line with a small train of empty wagons in 1962. This is the locomotive that came to the UK in 1967, to become the FR "Mountaineer". (AMTP / J.F.Organ coll.)

Musée des Transports de Pithiviers

Following its formation in 1965, the Association du Musée des Transports de Pithiviers (AMTP) began discussions with higher authority for their proposed preservation of at least part of this historic tramway. Ultimately a 4km section of the route between Pithiviers and Bellebat was saved along with the extensive works and station complex at the former location, which was re-opened on 23rd April 1966. Three of the former TPT locomotives were acquired by the AMTP in addition to one from the Toury refinery system. To these they have added an extensive collection of characteristic machines from other lines that succumbed to closure during the 1960s. In addition to the working fleet of five steam locomotives, two diesel loco-tractors and the pioneer railcar, the remainder of the extensive collection is displayed in a comprehensive museum that occupies the former goods shed. The large workshop and depot complex has been retained for its original purpose.

Although not passing through spectacular scenery, a journey along this mainly roadside tramway is not without interest. Leaving the beautifully restored station, situated on the western edge of Pithiviers, the route initially passes alongside the workshops before descending on a 1in 45 gradient in order to pass under the SNCF freight only branch line that runs between Orléans and Malesherbes. It then bears to the left and negotiates two level crossings over minor roads and another over a standard gauge siding leading to a fertiliser factory. The line now adopts its roadside position as it climbs towards the plateau at Ormes, which is now dominated by a recent addition to the landscape in the form of the Pithiviers by-pass that crosses the railway and road on a lofty bridge. At Ormes the line deviates from the original route to the purpose built terminus at Bellebat, where a replica of a typically French country station has been constructed. Originally, the outer terminus comprised of a simple loop and turning triangle. During the 1990s, however, the latter was replaced with a large turning circle which allows for a far more flexible operating arrangement to be implemented.

With its comprehensive stock of locomotives and rolling stock, including the items displayed in the museum, the AMTP is one of the most interesting preserved lines in France. With its roadside running line and fully developed complexes at each terminus, it is full of interest despite its short length. The active steam locomotives currently are a Blanc-Misseron 0-6-0T, Franco-Belge 0-8-0T (both ex TPT), Henschel Feldbahn variant 0-8-0T, La Meuse 2-6-0T and Decauville 0-6-2T. The principal exhibits in the museum are a diminutive Schneider 0-4-0T, two Decauville Type Progrès 0-4-0Ts and a 0-6-0T (ex Toury refinery), Hartmann Feldbahn 0-8-0T and ALCO 2-6-2T (ex TPT). In addition there is a metre gauge Cail 2-6-0T whilst the 1922 Crochat railcar is preserved in working order and makes occasional forays along the line. Only one of the former TPT carriages has survived into preservation. The remaining passenger stock is comprised of five replica Decauville carriages built on the frames of freight wagons, together with four trailer cars from the Valenciennes Tramway. The majority of the locomotives, railcar and the original carriage are listed as Monument Historique status items. However, being a wholly volunteer organisation, operations are limited to Sundays and Bank Holidays between May and October, with additional services on Saturdays during July and August.

Pithiviers is situated 80km south-west of Paris and 40km north-east of Orléans.

1.3 The first locomotive to work on the revived railway in 1966 was this Blanc-Misseron 0-6-0T. The TPT had used their own individual numbering system, which incorporated a prefix indicating the number of coupled axles followed by a running number, as shown in this view of no.3-5 inside the depot at Pithiviers on 3rd August 2013. (T.Kautzor)

1.4   Franco-Belge 0-8-0T no.4-12 was seen outside the depot whilst being prepared for duty on 9th September 1996. This view clearly shows the additional tanks fitted alongside the smokebox, when it was converted from its original 0-8-0 form in 1945. (J.F.Organ)

1.5   In addition to the steam locomotives, the AMTP also has a small collection of diesel powered machines for emergency use and shunting duties. Gmeinder 0-6-0D no.T11 was viewed at Pithiviers whilst engaged in the latter activity on 22nd July 2001. (J.F.Organ)

1.6 To celebrate their 20th anniversary, FACS ran a special steam hauled train to Pithiviers via the freight only branch line from Orléans on 8th May 1977. 4-6-0 no.G353 was pictured on the bridge above the AMTP tracks whilst La Meuse 2-6-0T no.9 passed below en-route to the narrow gauge station. (AMTP /J.F.Organ coll)

1.7   Decauville 0-6-2T no.10 was photographed at the beautifully restored station, prior to departure with a train bound for Bellebat on 20th June 2008. (R.M.Cable)

1.8   The same locomotive was photographed as it passed the industrial outskirts of Pithiviers during the early stages of the journey on 14th August 1994. (J.F.Organ)

1.9   0-8-0T no. 4-12 was recorded as it left Pithiviers and began the climb towards the plateau, whilst hauling a train comprised of the four former Valenciennes carriages. This view was obtained in September 1995. (AMTP / J.F.Organ coll)

1.10   At a nearby location, La Meuse 2-6-0T no.9 was viewed as it traversed the now unused standard gauge level crossing on 8th September 2013. (T.Kautzor)

1.11   0-6-2T no.10 was witnessed as it attacked the climb towards the plateau whilst en-route to Bellebat on 14th August 1994. (J.F.Organ)

1.12 The flat landscape of Loiret is shown to advantage in this scene featuring Blanc-Misseron 0-6-0T no. 3-5 as it approached Ormes, whilst hauling a rake of replica Decauville carriages in September 1995. (AMTP / J.F.Organ coll.)

1.13. Decauville 0-6-2T no.10 was photographed whilst running round its train at Bellebat on 14th August 1994. This class of locomotive was known as the Type Royan, as used at the pioneer Decauville Tramway at Royan in the 1890s, although this example was constructed in 1902. (J.F.Organ)

1.14   Also engaged in the running round operation was Franco-Belge 0-8-0T no.4-12, when it was recorded at Bellebat on 9th September 1996. (J.F.Organ)

1.15   One of the ubiquitous Feldbahn 0-8-0Ts, which are a prominent feature of the majority of French 600mm gauge railways. Henschel no.4 was seen whilst resting between duties at Bellebat on 22nd July 2001. (J.F.Organ)

1.16   Following its lunchtime break, the 1917 built 0-8-0T was coupled to the carriages and is awaiting the guards signal to depart for the return journey. (J.F.Organ)

1.17   The replica station building at Bellebat forms the backdrop of this scene featuring 2-6-0T no.9, as it arrived at the upper terminus on 8th September 2013. (T.Kautzor)

1.18   The same train was viewed as it made a circuit of the turning circle at Bellebat, which was completed in 1995. (T.Kautzor)

1.19   During the return journey, no.9 was flagged across one of the level crossings on the approach to Pithiviers. The main advantage of the mainly roadside location of the AMTP is that it allows for photography of the same train in a variety of settings, as shown in this September 2013 view. (T.Kautzor)

1.20   Back at Pithiviers station, 0-6-2T no.10 had just arrived at the platform when it was recorded on 20th June 2008. (R.M.Cable)

1.21   0-8-0T no. 4-12 had just uncoupled and was running forward prior to running round behind the station building. This view from 9th September 1996 clearly shows the cradle supporting the additional side tanks at the front of the locomotive. (J.F.Organ)

1.22   Inside the museum, ALCO 2-6-2T no.3-22 was displayed in a prime position when it was seen on 3rd August 2013. (T.Kautzor)

1.23   The diminutive Schneider 0-4-0T is occasionally allowed out of the museum, along with its equally diminutive carriage, as recorded in September 2013. (T.Kautzor)

1.24   Another active exhibit in the museum is the 1922 Crochat Petrol-Electric railcar no.AT1. It was photographed during a visit to Froissy on 6th May 2016. (C.Walker)

2. FROISSY – CAPPY – DOMPIERRE
(Le P'tit Train de la Haute Somme)

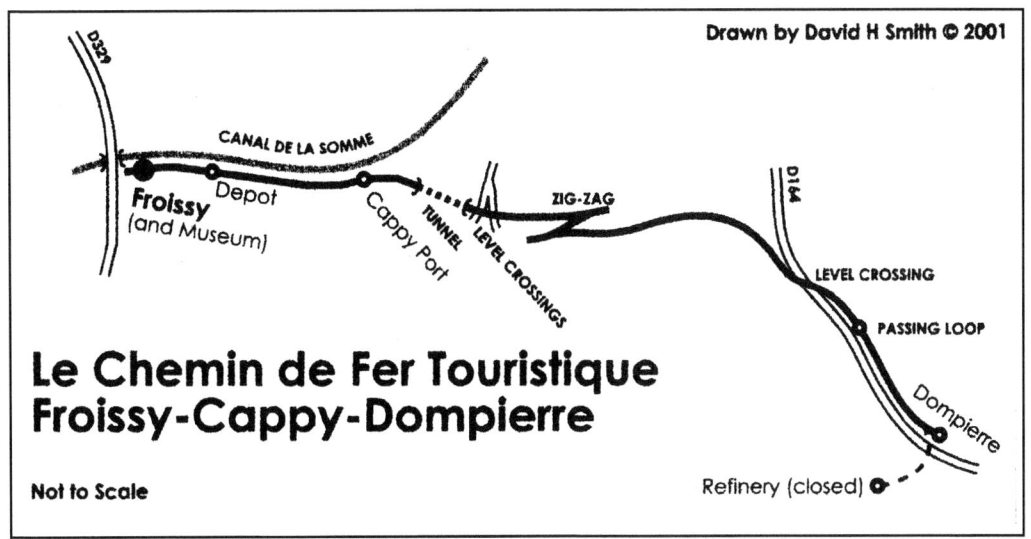

III. The CFCD in its present form is depicted in this sketch. Originally the route continued for many kilometres beyond Dompierre. (D.H.Smith)

This now very successful tourist railway owes its origins to the dark days of WWI. In 1915 the French army constructed a 600mm gauge supply line alongside the Somme Canal between Froissy and Cappy. The following year with the escalation of hostilities in the Battle of the Somme, Cappy was to find itself close to the front line, with the use of this railway adapted to great effect by the Allies. The German army was established above the village on the Santerre Plateau and constructed their own 600mm gauge Feldbahn system – both lines transporting a huge amount of ammunition and equipment on a daily basis as the war continued for another two years with neither side gaining any appreciable advantage.

Following the Armistice in 1918, the two railways were connected in order to be used in the clearance of wartime debris and for reconstruction. The connecting line involved a steep incline between the village and the plateau, which restricted the number of wagons that could be hauled. In 1927, after the majority of the reconstruction work had been completed, the line was taken over by the sugar refinery at Dompierre, whilst a quarry and brickworks also made use of the system. At this time, the steep incline was replaced by a new route which by-passed Cappy village via a 300metre long tunnel and a 1 in 33 climb through woodland to the plateau. In order to ease the gradient a "zig-zag" reversing section was incorporated into the new route, a feature which still remains today. Various extensions were constructed beyond Dompierre, although these were all closed by 1954. The line continued its unassuming role in conveying the products of the refinery and quarry to the canal wharf at Cappy-Port until 1972, when road transport became a cheaper option before the refinery was closed in 1988.

2.1 A World War One scene was re-enacted outside the loco-shed at Froissy with a trio of visiting locomotives to mark the centenary of the Battle of the Somme. The Simplex 4wPD and Baldwin 2-4-0DM from the Ffestiniog Railway were viewed alongside Baldwin 4-6-0T no.778 from Leighton Buzzard on 6th May 2016. (D.Blondin)

2.2　　The two Ffestiniog locomotives were recorded outside the museum with a WWI military train, complete with authentic personnel on the same date. (P.Dubocq / APPEVA)

2.3　　The Baldwin 2-4-0DM was witnessed as it passed the carriage shed whilst hauling a French military train, including the replica pre-WWI carriage. (P.Dubocq / APPEVA)

Preservation

In 1970, an organisation, known as L'Association Picarde pour la Preservation et L' Entretien des Vehicules Anciens (APPEVA), was formed with the intention of finding a suitable home for the collection of locomotives and rolling stock they were acquiring. The location at Froissy offered an ideal solution for their purposes, being situated mid-way between Paris and Lille and within easy reach of Amiens in an area popular with visitors and tourists. The Chemin de Fer Froissy-Cappy-Dompierre (CFCD) soon became an accepted part of the French preservation scene and continues to prosper.

Initially only the 1km of track alongside the canal between Froissy and Cappy was available, the first train being operated in June 1971. Following the arrival of more stock and the final closure of the upper sections of the line, APPEVA were able to access the entire 7km route in 1974, although the section along the plateau was not reinstated until 1976 following improvements to the permanent way and the two level crossings. Since then, the CFCD has developed into one of the most highly respected tourist railways in France, boasting a vast array of locomotives and rolling stock. In 1996, to celebrate the 25th anniversary of APPEVA, an impressive new museum and station complex was opened at Froissy, incorporating a semi-roundhouse and turntable. The adjacent original depot and carriage shed were retained for use as the engineering base for the railway. At this time, the CFCD's operating name was changed to Le P'tit Train de la Haute Somme et son Musée des C.F.Militaires & Industriels, although it is still more commonly referred to by its original name.

The formidable collection of locomotives is formed with examples from the French industrial and agricultural lines, including a brace of ubiquitous Decauville Type Progrès 0-6-0Ts. WWI is also represented by two Feldbahn 0-8-0Ts with examples from Krauss and Borsig, the latter in fact being modified to 0-8-0TT configuration. For many years they were joined by a former Pithiviers ALCO 2-6-2T, which was sadly sold by its owner in 2013 to a new location south of Paris. However the Allied contribution to the war effort is still represented by Baldwin and Simplex loco-tractors. The most powerful machines at Froissy are a 1925 built Vulcan 0-8-0, which originally worked in north-east Germany at the Mecklenburg-Pommerche Bahn and a 1945 Franco-Belge 0-8-0TT which, unlike its contemporaries at the TPT, still retains its tender. Locomotives awaiting restoration include an O & K 0-10-0T, which for many years was part of the TPT stock at Pithiviers. The industrial history of the CFCD is represented by two of the Coferna diesel locomotives and a smaller Plymouth loco-tractor, whilst a 1980s Romanian Faur diesel locomotive has been added to the collection in recent years. Rolling stock comprises mainly "home built" carriages constructed on the frames of former freight wagons, some of which are of WWI origin. In 2016 a replica pre-WWI French Army carriage was completed at Froissy. As with the AMTP collection at Pithiviers, many of the locomotives have been granted Monument Historique status.

The regular pattern of operation consists of a steam hauled trip alongside the canal between Froissy and Cappy-Port. Here, if one of the smaller locomotives is in use, steam haulage gives way to diesel power for the climb through the tunnel and the interesting negotiation of the "zig-zag" reversal section. At the summit of the climb the line crosses the road via an un-gated level crossing and adopts a roadside location along the plateau to the outskirts of Dompierre. Originally the line re-crossed the road to terminate alongside the sugar refinery. Since the closure of the refinery, this final short section has been closed, thus eliminating the level crossing at the upper terminus. The return journey incorporates a visit to the superb and well displayed museum, which is well worth a visit in its own right. When one of the larger steam locomotives is in use, the entire journey is steam hauled, which is an occurrence of great delight for the passengers!

In addition to operating the CFCD, APPEVA are also publishers of *Voie Etroite* the leading French magazine devoted to heritage railways, the sales of which provide some much needed additional revenue towards the running costs of the railway. The CFCD is twinned with the Leighton Buzzard Railway and enjoys close links with the Ffestiniog Railway. During a major event in 2016 to mark the centenary of the Battle of the Somme and the 45th anniversary of APPEVA, representative motive power from both the LBR and FR plus the West Lancs Railway were in attendance.

Like the majority of wholly volunteer run operations, services are normally restricted to Sundays and Bank Holidays between May and October, whilst the peak summer season in July and August sees additional daily diesel hauled trains – except Mondays. Froissy is approximately 25km east of Amiens, near Bray-sur-Somme and Albert.

2.4   Borsig 0-8-0TT no.7 was photographed at the lower terminus station at Froissy, prior to hauling a train bound for Dompierre on 25th August 1996. (J.F. Organ)

2.5   ALCO 2-6-2T no.9, formerly TPT no.3-20, was recorded on the turntable outside the museum complex along with a Socofer diesel locomotive in August 1996. (J.F.Organ)

2.6   Borsig no.7 and Vulcan 0-8-0 no.8 were viewed outside the loco-shed whilst being prepared for service on 16th May 1996. (P.Johnson)

2.7   Former Toury Refinery Decauville Type Progrès 0-6-0T no.5 was seen from the viewing platform at the museum during the celebrations of May 2016. (C.Walker)

2.8   Kerr Stuart 0-6-0T "Joffre", visiting from the West Lancs Railway made an interesting comparison with the Decauville. The British built locomotives were built to basically the same design as the French machines. (C.Walker)

2.9   With the Somme Canal in the background, Vulcan 0-8-0 no.8 was recorded as it drew away from the works complex. It was en-route to Cappy and Dompierre during the Somme event on 8th May 2016. (C.Walker)

2.10   Fresh from overhaul and painted in works grey livery, the Vulcan 0-8-0 was viewed as it approached Cappy Port in October 2014. (J-M.Royon / APPEVA)

2.11   The Borsig 0-8-0TT had just arrived at Cappy Port with a well patronised train, when it was photographed on 25th August 1996. (J.F.Organ)

2.12   ALCO 2-6-2Ts no.9 and "Mountaineer" from the Ffestiniog, ex TPT nos 3-20 and 3-23 respectively, were seen together at Cappy on 16th May 1996. (P.Johnson)

2.13   The Vulcan was witnessed as it emerged from the tunnel at Cappy and immediately crossed a minor road. Although the 0-8-0 is no.8 in the CFCD roster, it was carrying its original MPSB no.9 when photographed during September 2015. (D.Blondin)

2.14 The Franco-Belge 0-8-0TT no.10 and Vulcan 0-8-0 were hauling freight trains, whilst Coferna Diesel no.T25 waited in the loop, at the lower junction on the "Zig-Zag" section on the occasion of an enthusiast day in October 2014. (D.Blondin)

2.15   The Vulcan 0-8-0 was viewed as it climbed steadily away from the upper junction of the "Zig-Zag" on 6th May 2016. (D.Blondin)

2.16   The CFCDs most powerful locomotive is the Franco-Belge 0-8-0TT. The 1945 built machine was recorded as it climbed from the woodland and onto the Santerre Plateau in September 2015. (D.Blondin)

2.17   Coferna no.T25 had just crossed the road along the plateau and was beginning the descent towards Cappy with a passenger train on the same occasion in 2015. (D.Blondin)

2.18 At the conclusion of the Somme centenary event, an evening special train for staff and volunteers was hauled by the two visiting Baldwin locomotives. The interesting combination was recorded at the plateau passing loop on 8th May 2016. (D.Blondin)

2.19 The Vulcan and Franco-Belge machines were posed alongside each other, at the head of their respective freight trains, at the plateau loop in October 2014. (D.Blondin)

2.20   An earlier view of the Vulcan 0-8-0 was seen at Dompierre terminus during 1996. At that time it still carried its DR number 99 3461. (APPEVA / J.F.Organ coll.)

2.21   At the same location, the Franco-Belge KDL type 0-8-0 had just arrived with a freight train in October 2014. This view of the locomotive, restored to its original condition, makes an interesting comparison to those of the same class that were converted to 0-8-0Ts at Pithiviers in 1945. (D.Blondin)

2.22   The recently completed replica French Army carriage was viewed at Froissy, during its inauguration to service on 6th May 2016. (C.Walker)

2.23   Krauss Feldbahn 0-8-0T no.4 was displayed inside the recently completed museum, when it was seen on 25th August 1996. (J.F.Organ)

2.24 The interior of the impressive and spacious museum was recorded from the internal viewing platform in September 2015. In the foreground is a Baldwin 0-4-0PM whilst another Feldbahn 0-8-0T can be seen in the left background. (D.Blondin)

3. CHEMIN de Fer FORESTIER D'ABRESCHVILLER

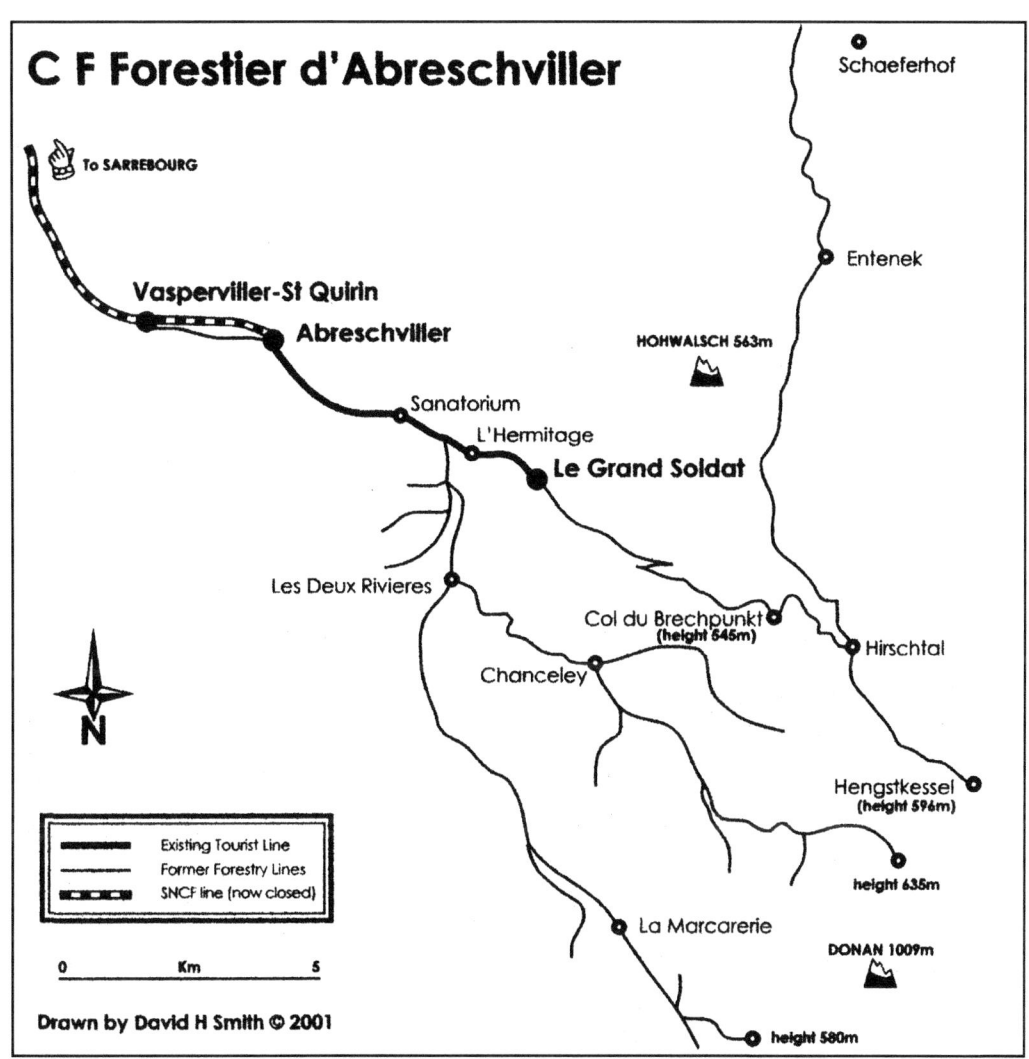

IV. The full extent of the CFA network is shown in this map. The surviving tourist line traverses a very small section of this once vast system. (D.H.Smith)

Following the Franco-Prussian war of 1870-71, much of north eastern France in Alsace and Lorraine was transferred to German administration, a situation that continued until after the Armistice in 1918. This had a lasting effect, which remains to this day with cultural and architectural features that bear a definite Germanic influence.

During the period of German control, the enormous areas of forest near Abreschviller, in the Vosges hills to the north west of Strasbourg, were exploited for commercial use. In 1884 a 700mm gauge railway system was constructed in order to transport the timber from the felling sites to the saw mills at Abreschviller. At its maximum extent the system had a total distance of 73km, plus additional temporary tracks to the felling areas which added a further 25km to the network. Two violent storms in 1892 and 1902 brought down vast numbers of trees, which provided added incentive to develop the operation.

Due to the location at the time of its construction in Germany, not surprisingly equipment from that source was used for this railway. The chosen gauge of 700mm was, at that time, in use for the German military railways. However there is no indication that it was ever intended for military use! As a consequence, the initial motive power was provided by small locomotives supplied by O & K, whilst from 1906 the principal workhorse was a 0-4-4-0T Mallet built by Heilbronn. In 1928, after the area was returned to French administration, the Mallet was joined by a Decauville Type Progrès 0-6-0T. Both of these machines are still in use at the railway, along with two small railcars built in the workshops at Abreschviller in 1925 and 1930 based on Renault and Hotchkiss motor vehicles. A notable feature of the working practice of this railway was the use of very long coupling poles between the wagons. This was necessary in view of the full length tree trunks transported on double bolster trucks, combined with the excessive curvature of the route through the forest. The railway finally closed in 1966, another victim of competition from road transport.

3.1 The Decauville 0-6-0T was viewed as it hauled a well loaded train of timber from the forest, whilst en-route to Abreschviller during the late 1950s. (ACFA coll.)

3.2 The sinuous nature of the line, and the need of long coupling poles, was emphasised in this view of the Coferna diesel locomotive as it hauled another train towards the saw mills during the final decade of the commercial operation. (ACFA coll.)

Regrettably, colour images were not available for this era.

From Timber to Tourism

Prior to the closure of the forestry railway in 1966 a number of enthusiast special trains were run, with the participants seated on benches placed in open wagons. The success of these, together with the scenic attractions of the area, provided the incentive for the creation of a tourist operation on part of the system. Although much of the track bed within the forests was in the process of being converted into roads, the lower 6km of the route between Abreschviller and the hamlet of Grand-Soldat was retained. With the co-operation of FACS and the local Département, the line was transferred to the newly formed Association du Chemin de Fer Forestier d'Abreschviller (ACFA) in June 1968.

The journey along this interesting railway begins at Abreschviller where the former goods shed has been transformed into an attractive station, which contains the customary shop and small museum. Alongside, is the fully equipped workshop and depot, whilst the nearby former sawmills have been converted into an art gallery and a restaurant. Leaving the station, the line initially runs below the town alongside a minor road, before entering the first sections of woodland. Following a series of tight curves, the passing place at Rommelstein is reached. Almost immediately the River Sarre Rouge is crossed on a steel and timber bridge, which is followed by a level crossing. There then begins a steep climb, including a gradient of 1 in 15, to Grand-Soldat after which another short section of roadside formation leads to the upper terminus. Here, time is allowed for a visit to an excellent museum devoted to the railway and the timber industry, which includes a fascinating film showing the system operating in its hey-day.

The ACFA were able to acquire the remaining locomotives from the original company. These include the Heilbronn 0-4-4-0 Mallet, the Decauville 0-6-0T plus two diesel powered machines, a 1953 built Coferna and a smaller Deutz. In addition the two small Renault and Hotchkiss based railcars were added to the collection, whilst one of the original smaller O & K 0-4-0Ts is on static display a Grand-Soldat. Within a short period, the venture proved to be highly successful to the extent that additional motive power was required. This was provided by the acquisition of a Jung HF110C 0-6-0TT built in 1944 for the German military railways and subsequently used in Austria at Stainz. Following its purchase in 1975, this 760mm gauge locomotive was re-gauged at the Abreschviller workshops in order to operate on the 700mm track and has since proved to be an excellent addition to the stock, being by far the most powerful locomotive on the railway. The passenger stock is comprised of a number of open sided carriages built on the frames of former freight wagons, whilst more comfortable accommodation is provided by closed vehicles acquired from the Wengernalpbahn in Switzerland and a former German military railway at Donon.

Situated 70km north-west of Strasbourg and 15km south of Sarrebourg, this excellent railway is well worth a visit. Despite its short length, it has much to offer in respect of its scenic attractions and the history of the original system. Operations are mainly at weekends and bank holidays between May and October, with a daily service during July and August.

3.3   The Renault and Hotchkiss railcars were posed alongside the Heilbronn Mallet when seen outside the loco-shed at Abreschviller in June 2007. (D.Huntbatch)

3.4   At the same location, the Jung 0-6-0TT and the Mallet were both receiving their final preparations prior to service during August 2014. (N.Moser)

3.5　The Deutz shunting locomotive was recorded as it hauled a rake of former lumberjack wagons from the siding alongside the station on 4th June 2016. (N.Moser)

3.6　Shortly after re-entering service following an overhaul, the Jung HF 110C 0-6-0TT was photographed as it began a journey to Grand-Soldat in August 2014. (N.Moser)

3.7   Many of the trains are diesel hauled, especially during the mid week period. The 1953 built Coferna was viewed as it passed the lower part of the town during the early stages of its journey to the forest on 31st August 2006. (J.F.Organ)

3.8   A re-enactment of a forestry workers train, but with children instead of lumberjacks, was staged on 4th June 2016. The ensemble was recorded as it ran through the lower part of the forest near Rommelstein. (N.Moser)

3.9   Another train hauled by the Coferna diesel locomotive was seen as it approached the level crossing beyond Romelstein during August 2014. (N.Moser)

3.10   The more powerful Jung 0-6-0TT was attacking the steep incline on the final ascent towards Grand-Soldat, when it was witnessed in August 2014. (N.Moser)

3.11 A few minutes later, the same train was photographed as it crossed the minor road in the hamlet of Grand-Soldat, before the final climb to the upper terminus. (N.Moser)

3.12   The Decauville 0-6-0T was recorded as it coupled onto its carriages at Grand-Soldat. The retired O & K 0-4-0WT can be seen in the background, on its plinth alongside the museum, in this scene from June 2005. (N.Moser)

3.13   The small station at Grand-Soldat can be seen in this view of the Heilbronn Mallet, which had just arrived with a train from Abreschviller in June 2007. (D.Huntbatch)

3.14 The compact design of the Jung 110C locomotives is very apparent in this view from August 2014. These locomotives were supplied for the 750mm German field railways during WWII by many constructors such as Jung and Henschel. (N.Moser)

3.15   The timber clad water tank at the upper terminus is featured in this view of the German 0-6-0TT replenishing its water supply on the same occasion in 2014. (N.Moser)

3.16   The attractive surroundings of Grand-Soldat form the backdrop to this scene as the diesel hauled train arrives at the station, whilst the Jung awaits departure for the return journey in August 2014. (N.Moser)

4. CHEMIN de Fer de la VALLÉE de L'OUCHE

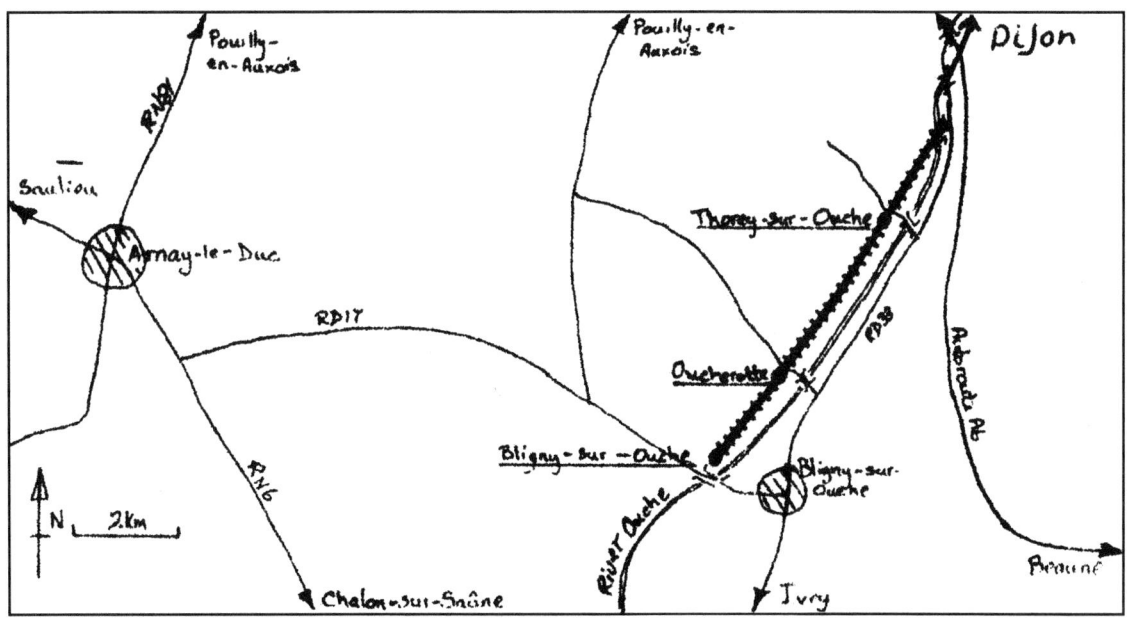

V. The short route of the CFVO, in relation to its location in Burgundy, is shown in this sketch of the line. (R.Hayworth)

In reality, this 600mm gauge railway is not a historic survivor. However the track bed on which it operates is most definitely part of French railway history. In 1839 this standard gauge line was opened between Epinac and Port d'Ouche and was one of the first railways in France. Its initial purpose was to transport coal from the mines near Epinac to the Canal de Bourgogne, horses providing the original motive power. Ultimately the line became part of the SNCF network until it was closed in 1970.

At about that time, the local authorities were considering the development of leisure activities in the area in an attempt to promote tourism, and a tourist railway was considered to be an ideal attraction for this scheme. As the former PLM/SNCF station at Bligny sur Ouche was still in good condition, this was considered to be the obvious choice from which to start the project. 7.2km of track bed to the north of Bligny was purchased, whilst the station area at the headquarters were developed into a well laid out complex incorporating a workshop and locomotive shed, with the station building containing the booking office, shop and offices.

600mm was the chosen gauge for the new railway in view of the availability of motive power and rolling stock. Following the preparatory and construction work the CF de la Vallée de L'Ouche (CFVO) began operations in 1978. The first president of the railway was the late Jean-Claude Laboureau, who was also well known as a volunteer fireman on the Ffestiniog Railway with his frequent visits to North Wales. Initially only 5km of track was available; this was ultimately extended to the northern terminus beyond Thorey sur Ouche. During the last three decades, the CFVO has developed into one of the principal tourist railways of France and a major attraction in this part of Burgundy. Some useful publicity for the line was promoted in 1995 when Jean-Claude Laboureau took the Krauss Feldbahn locomotive to the Ffestiniog Railway to participate in a major gala.

A good working relationship has been developed with the AMTP at Pithiviers and the CFTM at Montalieu (see Chapter Six). During the early period of the CFVO operation, two locomotives were obtained on loan from the latter organisation, one of which was subsequently purchased. At that time the CFVO only owned one locomotive, a Decauville 0-4-0TT built in 1947 to a Henschel design. This was joined by the two CFTM machines, a Krauss Feldbahn 0-8-0T and a Couillet 0-6-0T, which originally worked at the Maizy sugar refinery near Rheims. The Couillet was purchased from CFTM in 1999, whilst the Krauss was returned to Montalieu in 2002. In return the CFVO obtained two locomotives from the CFTM stock. These were former Maizy refinery no.8, a La Meuse 2-6-0T of 1938 vintage, and an ex Pithiviers Franco-Belge KDL type 0-8-0T built in 1945, both of which were in need of major overhauls. The La Meuse was rebuilt at Pithiviers, where sister locomotive no.9 is a long term resident, and was returned to service at Bligny in May 2008. The Franco-Belge machine no.4.13 has recently been sold to APEMVE, a preservation group based in the Sarthe area of Central France.

Due to its location on a former standard gauge route, the CFVO is devoid of some of the acute curvature and steep gradients often associated with narrow gauge lines. It does however pass through picturesque countryside, and the infrastructure and equipment are maintained in excellent condition. Bligny sur Ouche is a delightful typically French village, situated 20km west of Beaune and 52km south of Dijon. Steam hauled trains operate on Sundays and Bank Holidays from 1st May until 30th September, whilst a diesel hauled service operates daily during July and August.

4.1 The tree enshrouded station at Bligny was the setting for this view of the 0-4-0TT Decauville / Henschel locomotive as it was about to depart for a journey along the line on 5th September 2003. (R.M.Cable)

4.2   The Couillet 0-6-0T was recorded following its arrival at the station, whilst the last passengers admire the immaculate locomotive on 15th August 2003. (R.M.Cable)

4.3   The former PLM/SNCF station building forms the backdrop of this scene, as the Couillet 0-6-0T prepared to return to the depot on the same occasion. (R.M.Cable)

4.4 The two locomotives were viewed outside the impressive depot and workshop complex during the same day in August 2003. (R.M.Cable)

4.5 Following its extensive restoration at Pithiviers, La Meuse 2-6-0T no.8 was recorded arriving at Bligny, during the course of one of its first days of operation in May 2008.
(The late J-C Laboureau)

4.6 The Decauville 0-4-0TT, built in 1947 to a Henschel design, was drifting towards the station when it was viewed on 5th September 2003. (R.M.Cable)

4.7   For its return to service, 2-6-0T no.8 was joined by Blanc-Misseron 0-6-0T no.3.5 from Pithiviers. The two locomotives, in matching livery, were witnessed at the intermediate station at Thorey-sur-Ouche during May 2008. (The late J-C Laboureau)

4.8   The Decauville/Henschel 0-4-0TT was photographed as it departed from the upper terminus beyond Thorey-sur-Ouche on 15th September 2003. (R.M.Cable)

5. CHEMIN de Fer TOURISTIQUE du TARN

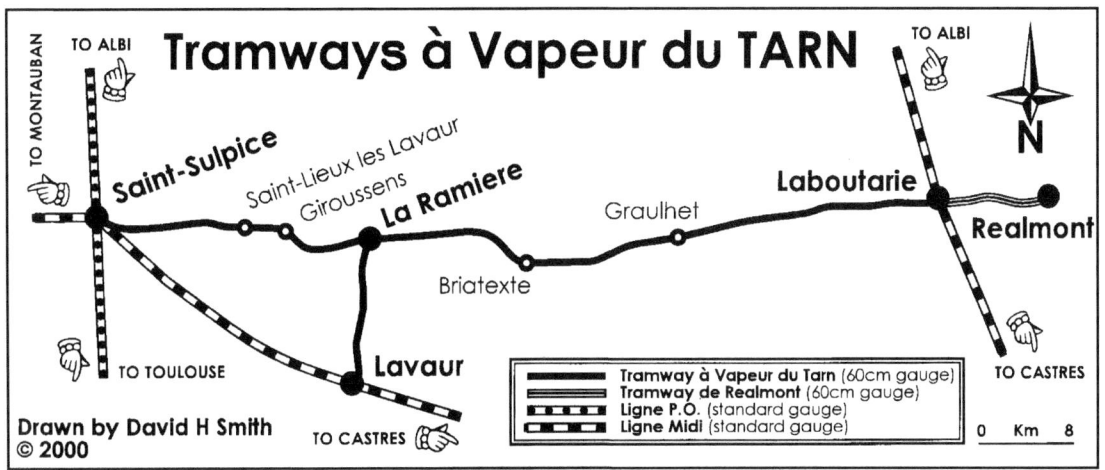

VI. The original route of the TVT is shown in this map. The current CFTT operation is confined to a short section near the western end of the former system. (D.H.Smith)

Although the majority of the surviving sub-metre railways are located in the northern half of France, one notable survivor is situated in the south of the country near Toulouse. The C.F.T. du Tarn (CFTT) has its origins in an extensive 600mm gauge system known as Tramways à Vapeur du Tarn, which was located near Toulouse and Castres, and operated between 1895 and 1937. Castres was also better known as the principal station and headquarters of the impressive metre gauge CFD du Tarn until its demise in 1962.

Although much of the Tarn Tramway had been lost to nature and re-development, following its closure in 1937, the station at the village of St. Lieux-les-Lavaur had survived but this too was under the threat of demolition in 1975. At this point a group of determined enthusiasts based in Toulouse stepped in and acquired the station site and also a section of track bed to the east of the village. They also obtained consent to relay the roadside track through the village and across the nearby six arch viaduct. The next stage of the operation by the newly formed Le Association pour la Conservation Occitane de Vehicules Anciens (ACOVA) was to obtain suitable track and equipment. A workshop and depot facility was constructed between the village and viaduct in order to overhaul and maintain the stock they were acquiring for use on the CFTT.

By that stage, very little 600mm gauge stock was available, but they were able to buy a 500mm gauge Decauville 0-4-0T, so consequently the decision was made to relay the track to the smaller gauge. In addition the Decauville was subsequently joined between 1987 and 1998 by three more examples of this classic French design. Three former military Crochat petrol-electric loco-tractors of WWI vintage were also acquired, together with some industrial diesel powered machines. To bolster the stock of steam locomotives, a Couillet 0-6-0T of 1910 vintage (ex. Maizy refinery and sister of the Couillet at Bligny) was purchased from AMTP at Pithiviers in 1985. As with the afore mentioned Crochat machines, this 600mm gauge locomotive required re-gauging before it could operate at its new home. The rolling stock consists of a fleet of bogie carriages built at the CFTT workshops using the frames of former industrial vehicles. Two of the carriages are based on Baguely units that were imported from Britain in 1977 and 1981.

The route of this 5km long tramway runs through a delightful pastoral landscape. After departing from the fully restored station at St. Lieux, with its small engine shed and a four-road layout, the line immediately traverses an un-gated level crossing over the road leading to Lavaur. There then follows a short section between the houses of the village before emerging in open countryside, where a spur leading to the workshop and depot complex has been constructed. The route then adopts a roadside alignment, which includes the section across the viaduct. After crossing the structure, the line leaves the road and passes through a rural area of fields and woodland before arriving at the outer terminus adjacent to a garden centre at La Masquière.

The CFTT station at St. Lieux is located 37km north-east of Toulouse and approximately the same distance to the north-west of Castres. The nearest town is St. Sulpice, which is 8km to the west. Trains operate on Sundays and Bank Holidays between Easter and October, with additional services (mainly diesel hauled) on Saturdays, Mondays and Tuesdays during July and August.

5.1 Decauville 0-4-0T no.3 was seen raising steam outside the small loco shed at St.Lieux-les-Lavaur, prior to the day's service on 30th August 1997. (J.F.Organ)

5.2 The compact and attractive station at St.Lieux is featured in this 1997 view of no.3, with one of the small diesel locomotives in the background. (J.F.Organ)

5.3 The former Maizy and Pithiviers Couillet 0-6-0T no.1 was in a siding at St.Lieux, when it was witnessed on 17th August 2013. (T. Kautzor)

5.4   Another of the CFTT Decauville 0-4-0Ts, no.4 was recorded prior to departure from St.Lieux on the same occasion in August 2013. (T.Kautzor)

5.5   A few minutes later, no.4 was about to cross the road as it departed from the station at the start of its journey. (T.Kautzor)

5.6 One of the most photographed locations on the CFTT is the section though the small village of St.Lieux-les-Lavaur. No.3 was viewed as it passed between the houses of this delightful hamlet on 30th August 1997. (J.F.Organ)

5.7   No.4 was witnessed as it approached the viaduct over the River Agout, the major civil engineering structure on the railway, in this August 2013 scene. (T.Kautzor)

5.8   A clearer view of the combined rail and road viaduct was obtained on the same occasion in 2013. (T.Kautzor)

5.9   With the hilltop village of Giroussens in the background, one of the Crochat petrol-electric locomotives was seen in action during the 1990s. (ACOVA coll.)

5.10 Deep in the rural countryside of Southern France, the two Decauville locomotives were recorded at the mid-way passing loop on 18th August 2013. (T.Kautzor)

5.11   The outer terminus at La Masquière was the location for this view of no.4 running around the carriages on the same day in August 2013. (T.Kautzor)

5.12   At the completion of the journey, the Decauville 0-4-0T was photographed as it crossed the road and entered the station at St.Lieux on 18th August 2013. (T.Kautzor)

6. THE "NEW" TOURIST RAILWAYS

During the last five decades, a great number of small railways have been constructed throughout France. These were constructed on virgin sites, mainly at leisure parks or adjacent to other tourist attractions. The majority employ diesel motive power, many of which are "steam outline" machines, hauling gaudy liveried rolling stock of no historical significance. However there are other splendid operations that have been instrumental in the preservation of historic locomotives and associated equipment, which have become as much part of the preservation movement as the historic railways. One of the first of these schemes was the CF de St.-Eutrope at Evry, near the southern outskirts of Paris, which was opened in 1978. Despite its location near the former Decauville factory and its plans to combine the railway with a museum devoted to the history of the works, sadly this was not to be. Due to the land being required for re-development of the area, this splendid railway was closed in 2003, much of its equipment now being located at some of the other lines covered in the following pages, which are the principal examples of historic importance among these newly created schemes.

CHEMIN de Fer du HAUTE-RHÔNE

This short railway near Lyon owes its origins to the first preservation scheme in France, which pre-dated the AMTP by eight years. In 1958 a group of Lyon based enthusiasts under the leadership of the indefatigable Jean Arrivetz began to acquire redundant 600mm gauge locomotives and rolling stock, mainly from the industrial and agricultural lines of Northern France. In order to provide a home for their acquisitions, the Chemin de Fer Touristique du Meyzieu (CFTM) was established at Meyzieu in the eastern outskirts of Lyon. Here, a short roadside tramway was laid to provide a working home for the collection of seven locomotives they had acquired, whilst passenger rolling stock was adapted from former freight wagons.

The short Mezieu line operated a weekend service between 1962 and 1970, when the encroaching and expanding suburbs of Lyon resulted in the site being requisitioned for building development. By that time, the CFTM were heavily involved in the operation of the metre gauge Vivarais Railway between Tournon and Lamastre. As a consequence the 600mm stock was placed in store at a secure location until a new home for the railway could be found. As recorded earlier, two of the locomotives were loaned to the CFVO at Bligny during this period.

In 1988 a suitable location for the railway was found at Montalieu, 60km east of Lyon on the banks of the Rhône. Here, a 4km long riverside formation was laid from Montalieu northwards to Pont-de-Sault Brénaz, near where the river has been dammed in connection with a hydro-electric scheme. The motive power is provided by a Decauville 0-6-0T and a Krauss Feldbahn 0-8-0T along with two small industrial Billard diesels in reserve. Passenger rolling stock is now provided by former Neuchâtel and Valenciennes Tramway carriages. An interesting former TPT 0-4-4-0T Mallet, no.22-5 built by O & K in 1905, is stored at Montalieu awaiting a major overhaul, this being one of the first locomotives to be used at Meyzieu in 1962.

The CFTM transferred the operation of the line to the CF du Haute-Rhône in 2004. The railway provides a service on Sundays between May and October plus a Saturday service during July and August. A recent innovation has been the introduction of a vélorail operation, which allows participants the opportunity to "cycle" along the line. This operates daily during the summer months at times when trains are not running.

6a.1 The lower terminus at Montalieu-Vallée Bleue is the location for this scene featuring Billard loco-tractor no.T1 awaiting departure on 23rd March 1989. (J.Wiseman)

6a.2 The Decauville 0-6-0T and a former Valenciennes carriage was viewed among the trees as it drew away from Montalieu on 5th June 1995. (J.Wiseman)

6a.3   Whilst retaining the CFVO insignia from its days operating at Bligny, the Krauss Feldbahn 0-8-0T no.743 was recorded as it was about to couple up to the carriages during May 2016. (F.Mottet)

6a.4   With its paintwork somewhat faded compared to its appearance at Porthmadog in 1995, the Krauss locomotive was pictured prior to departure on the same day. (F.Mottet)

6a.5 Seen on a bright spring day, the Billard hauled its rake of former tramway carriages towards the upper terminus on 23rd March 1989. (J.Wiseman)

6a.6   Situated alongside the River Rhône, the terminus at Pont-de-Sault Brénaz was viewed from an elevated position on the same occasion. (J.Wiseman)

6a.7   The Decauville 0-6-0T and the entire compliment of tramway carriages was recorded at the upper terminus during July 2006. Part of the hydro-electricity complex can be seen behind the leading vehicle. (The late J.Arrivetz)

CHEMIN de Fer des CHANTERAINES

In the north-west suburbs of Paris, near Gennevilliers, a leisure park was created during the 1970s at the instigation of the local authorities, close to the Ile St.Denis in the River Seine. As part of the scheme, a tourist railway was considered to be an added attraction. Consequently a 5.5km long 600mm gauge line was constructed in stages between 1984 and 1991.

The completed route follows a sinuous course including a spiral loop from a terminal station close to the Pont d'Epinay. The line initially follows the south bank of the Seine for 1.3km before curving sharp right into the park. It then climbs abruptly to cross the main road through the park on a long steel viaduct, before descending over the spiral loop. There then follows a section alongside a lake before crossing the A86 autoroute on a long concrete bridge, after which the line turns again to enter the outer terminus at Gennevilliers, where the well equipped depot and workshop are located.

The stock consists of five steam locomotives and seven diesel powered machines. The steam fleet includes a Decauville Type Progrès 0-6-0T dating from 1920, another Decauville in the form of a 0-4-0T built under license by Borsig in 1911 and a further German machine, an O & K 0-4-0WT of 1905 vintage. In addition, an O & K 0-6-0T and another Decauville 0-4-0T are in store awaiting overhaul. The diesel machines include examples of Plymouth, Campagne and Socofer, the latter concern having also constructed the rolling stock.

Noted for its immaculate state of presentation, this splendid railway located near the centre of Paris is well worth a visit. Operating days are between March and November, mainly on Saturdays, Sundays, Wednesdays and Bank Holidays.

6b.8 The familiar outline of a Decauville Type Progrès 0-6-0T was viewed as it posed ahead of a smaller Decauville / Borsig 0-4-0T outside the extensive workshop complex at Gennevilliers on 4th June 1994. (P.Johnson)

6b.9 Seen at the same location, the two resident locomotives were joined by visitors "Palmerston" from the Ffestiniog and 0-4-0TT no.1 from the CFVO. The small locomotive in the centre was a privately owned and built 15" gauge miniature based on the design of an O & K 0-4-0WT. (P.Johnson)

6b.10 The immaculate state of the infrastructure of this small railway is shown in this view of the Decauville 0-6-0T at the station at Gennevilliers in June 1994. (P.Johnson)

6b.11   Viewed during its holiday in France, "Palmerston" was recorded as it crossed the viaduct spanning the main road through the park on the same occasion. (P.Johnson)

6b.12   A large number of the trains at Chanteraines are hauled by one of the diesel locomotives, such as this Plymouth 4wDM viewed at the terminus near Pont d'Epinay, in another scene from 4th June 1994. (P.Johnson)

TACOT des LACS

Another railway within easy distance of Paris is located between Fontainebleu and Nemours, approximately 80km south of the capital. A project began in 1985 to construct a short tourist railway in which to operate a collection of locomotives that a group of enthusiasts were acquiring. The site chosen was a former sand pit situated near the River Loing and its adjacent canal. A running line with a total length of 2.5km has been constructed, whilst the large stock of material collected is mainly stored in a secure compound alongside the line. The working locomotives are housed in a depot near the principal intermediate station.

The route of the line begins alongside the canal at Montcourt before bearing away to the left towards the main station complex. There follows a short uphill section leading to a 35m long steel girder bridge across the river, which is followed by a short run to the outer terminus situated by the old sand workings. The girder bridge is in need of much needed attention, or even replacement. Consequently only the smaller locomotives are able to reach the upper section of the line at present.

The collection comprises a vast array of both steam and diesel motive power, the majority of which are in store awaiting restoration and too numerous to list in full. Among the working fleet are a number of small German built 0-4-0Ts of Borsig, Jung, Krauss and O & K origin together with an ubiquitous Decauville 0-4-0T. The larger machines include a brace of Henschel Feldbahn 0-8-0Ts, whilst the outstanding locomotive is a Baldwin 2-6-2T. This is one of a trio that worked at Penrhyn Quarry Railway during the 1920s where it was named "Felin-Hen" and is the lone survivor. Following a decade in store at Port Penrhyn it was exported to Australia in 1940 where it worked on a sugar plantation in Queensland, during which time it was much modified in appearance and ran as a 0-6-2T. The locomotive returned to France in 2005 and has since been rebuilt to its original condition and carrying its USA Army livery.

Also in the collection are three locomotives that were formerly based at Froissy. These were controversially sold by the widow of their former owner in 2013 and transferred to the Tacot line. Among these are the former WDLR and Pithiviers -Toury ALCO 2-6-2T, which many British enthusiasts will remember from its visit to Porthmadog in 1995.

This interesting, albeit short, railway operates at weekends and bank holidays between April and November, but not Saturdays in April and November, whilst a daily, mainly diesel, service is provided in July and August.

6c.13   Fully restored to its original condition following many years in Australia, former Penrhyn Quarry Railway Baldwin 2-6-2T "Felin-Hen" was viewed near the lower station during September 2013. (J.Waite)

6c.14   Proudly wearing its USA wartime livery, the Baldwin was recorded as it emerged from the depot complex on the same occasion. (J.Waite)

6c.15   Moments later and "Felin-Hen" was seen as it hauled a restored WWI wagon across the access road to the former sand pits. (J.Waite)

6c.16   Providing an interesting comparison with the Baldwin 2-6-2T, the former Pithiviers no.3-20 / CFCD no.9 ALCO 2-6-2T was pictured stored inside the depot during the same visit to this interesting railway in 2013. (J.Waite)

6c.17   Two of the former WWI Baldwin 0-4-0PM loco-tractors resident at the line were viewed in the storage compound on the same date. (J.Waite)

CHEMIN de Fer des COMBES

90km south-west of Dijon is the town of Le Creusot, famed for its large engineering and steel works complex. The major company is the long established Schneider group, which has produced items as diverse as armaments to some of the largest steam locomotives to have worked in France.

Above the town is a wooded hilltop area where a leisure park, known as Parc des Combes, was created during the 1980s. As part of this development, a 5km long 600mm gauge railway, encircling the highest part of the park, was constructed between 1989 and 1993. With steep gradients and severe horseshoe curves, continuous air braking has been fitted to the locomotives and stock. The lower section of this circuit incorporates part of the former standard gauge works railway including a short tunnel. During the last decade the length of the line has been doubled with the addition of a second steeply graded line that provides access to the SNCF station at Le Creusot. The result is an interesting and highly scenic journey through this park, which has many family and sporting attractions also on offer. The line has two depots, the working locomotives are based at a fully equipped shed and workshop near the station serving the original circuit, whilst the reserve stock and items awaiting the attention of the workshop are stored alongside the lower station.

Although steam haulage is featured at weekends, the majority of trains are diesel hauled with a daily service provided between March and November, which coincides with the opening days of the park. The weekend steam traction is normally restricted to the April to September period. The steam locomotives include two Henschel built Feldbahn 0-8-0Ts and a Decauville 0-6-0T whilst a newly restored O & K Feldbahn is awaiting service. One of the Henschels and the Decauville were acquired from the railway at St.-Eutrope when it closed in 2003. The diesel fleet is comprised of former industrial machines constructed by Berry, Billard, Deutz, Decauville and Plymouth. A journey on the railway is incorporated into a general admission ticket to the park or a train only ticket can also be obtained.

A museum devoted to the history of the Schneider organisation is also located at Le Creusot. The principal exhibit is a massive SNCF 4-8-2 no.241P17 which was built by Schneider in 1950. The des Combes line is the only railway featured in this album that is served by the SNCF network, via a cross country route between Dijon and Nevers.

6d.18   An early view of the Le Creusot operation featured their first Henschel Feldbahn being prepared for service outside the extensive depot in August 1994. This locomotive was sold to the Lac de Rillé line in 2014. (P.Pacey)

6d.19   Many of the trains are diesel hauled, notably during the mid-week period. One of the more powerful locomotives used for these services is this 120hp Plymouth 4wDM, seen on the same occasion. (P.Pacey)

6d.20   The lower station at Le Creusot has a spacious layout, as seen in this view of another Henschel 0-8-0T no.2, as it prepared to depart to the higher reaches of the line on 18th July 2007. (T.Kautzor)

6d.21 Henschel no.3, formerly resident at St-Eutrope, was overshadowed by the bulk of the former SNCF 4-8-2 no.241P17 when the two contrasting locomotives were witnessed alongside each other at Le Creusot on 23rd May 2010. (T.Kautzor)

6d.22 No.3 was recorded as it climbed away from the lower terminus during the ascent to the intermediate station on the same occasion. (T.Kautzor)

6d.23   The intermediate station was originally the lower terminus of the line, prior to the extensions of the last decade. Henschel no.2 was seen at the flag bedecked station on 18th July 2007. (T.Kautzor)

6d.24   The classic lines of the ubiquitous WWI Feldbahn design is shown to advantage in this view of Henschel no.2 alongside the water tower on the same date. (T.Kautzor)

← 6d.25 Shortly after leaving the station for the ascent of the upper circuit, the route passes through the tunnel of the former standard gauge mineral line. No.2 was recorded as it emerged from the portal before the climb to the summit section in July 2007. (T.Kautzor)

6d.26 No.3 was pictured at a passing loop, during the climb around the upper circuit on 23rd May 2010. (T.Kautzor)

6d.27   On the steepest section of the route, no.2 was witnessed as it climbed towards the summit on 18th July 2007. (T.Kautzor)

6d.28   An indication of the curvaceous route followed by the upper circuit can be appreciated by this elevated view of no.2 climbing the incline in July 2007. (T.Kautzor)

6d.29 No.2 was resting at the intermediate station before retiring to the depot at the conclusion of its duties on the same day in 2007. (T.Kautzor)

TRAIN TOURISTIQUE du LAC de RILLÉ

Located mid-way between Tours and Saumur, this 3km long railway at Rillé has operated at its present site since 1991. However its origins go back to 1977 when a group of enthusiasts created a depot at nearby Marcilly, in which to store the small collection of locomotives they had acquired. Their aim was to construct a short tourist railway on which to operate their stock. It soon became apparent that Marcilly was not the ideal location for such a venture, being situated away from the main tourist trails. After a decade of trials and tribulations, the enterprise was moved 12km to the south and re-located alongside the lake at Rillé, which was well established as a popular destination for both tourists and day visitors.

The route of the line begins at the principal station in the centre of the line, near the entrance to the leisure park alongside the car park and picnic area. From there the line runs along the southern shore of the lake until the outer terminus is reached adjacent to a causeway across the lake, although passengers are unable to join trains at this point. Returning to the main station, beyond there is a triangle followed by a circular section of track which also serves as access to the depot at the eastern end of the circuit. The depot area is dominated by the recently completed semi-roundhouse with five roads accessed by a turntable. Here are based all the working locomotives, in addition to those restored but not currently in use. The carriages and remaining items awaiting restoration are stored in a large building, where the workshops formerly at Marcilly have also been re-located. The carriages include items built at Marcilly plus two historic bogie coaches dating from 1890 and 1893, which began life as metre gauge vehicles on the CFD Indre-et-Loire and Réseau de l'Anjou systems respectively.

The two original locomotives restored at Marcilly are a 0-4-0WT built by O & K in 1913 and a 1917 Henschel Feldbahn 0-8-0TT, which was acquired from a forestry line in Poland where it was fitted with the tender that has been retained. These have been joined by two Decauville machines, including a 0-4-0T which was one of the last steam locomotives built by the company in 1947. The other Decauville is a 1916 built Type Progrès 0-6-0T, which is on loan from the proposed Decauville Museum at Evry, along with two diesel powered machines from the same establishment. A further Henschel Feldbahn 0-8-0T was purchased from the CF des Combes in 2014.

This small railway is also the home of arguably the largest 600mm gauge locomotive in France. This former 760mm gauge 0-8-0 tender engine was acquired from Romania in 2001 and re-gauged to 600mm shortly after its arrival. No.784-203 was built in 1949 at Bucharest and worked on the Romanian State Railway (CFR) 760mm gauge lines until retired at Tirgu Mires in 1996. When fully restored to service, this impressive locomotive will undoubtedly be in demand for guest appearances at other 600mm gauge railways.

The Lac du Rillé line operates at weekends between April and October, whilst a daily service is provided during August. This small friendly railway was twinned with the equally friendly West Lancs Railway, near Preston, in 2009. Rillé is located 35km from both Tours and Saumur.

6e.30   The first locomotive to be restored at Marcilly was this O & K 0-4-0WT. This classic design of German industrial locomotive was seen on the turntable alongside the semi-roundhouse, which was still under construction at the time that this view was captured on 15th September 2013. (P.Horton)

6e.31　The 0-4-0WT was witnessed as it approached the rolling stock of its train at the principal station, prior to a journey along the line on the same day. (P.Horton)

6e.32   Bedecked with French national flags, the Henschel Feldbahn 0-8-0TT was recorded as it ran off the triangle towards to station on 10th May 2015. (P.Horton)

6e.33   At a later stage of the journey, the 0-8-0TT was viewed as it drew away from the upper terminus. The tender added to the locomotives during its working life in Poland is clearly shown in this scene of May 2015. (P.Horton)

6e.34 During the course of another journey on the same date, the Henschel ran alongside the lake whilst en-route to the principal station. The locomotive had been turned and the flags removed prior to this photograph being obtained. (P.Horton)

Other Middleton Press publications of related interest to French Narrow Gauge Railways are *Vivarais Revisited* **(John Organ, 2007),** *Majorca and Corsica Narrow Gauge* **(John Organ, 2013) and** *French Metre Gauge Survivors* **(John Organ, 2016).**

6e.35 What must be the largest 600mm gauge locomotive in France, this former 760mm Romanian 0-8-0 was recorded whilst on display at the main station in June 2010, before its full restoration was completed. (J.David / P.Horton coll)

ENCORE

Although the locations of these small railways are not served by the SNCF network, with the exception of Le Creusot, they can all be reached by other forms of public transport. Due to this restricted accessibility and limited operating days, they do not feature in many organised tours such as those arranged by Ffestiniog Travel. However for anyone wishing to make an independent visit to one or more of these splendid lines, they can arrange the necessary tickets to the nearest railhead and accommodation. With easy access via the Channel Tunnel and the excellent TGV services throughout France, they can all be easily reached from the UK.

Ffestiniog Travel,
6 Snowdonia Business Park,
Minffordd, Gwynedd, LL486LD
Tel: 01766 772050   www: festtravel.co.uk

MP Middleton Press

EVOLVING THE ULTIMATE RAIL ENCYCLOPEDIA

Easebourne Midhurst GU29 9AZ. Tel:01730 813169

www.middletonpress.co.uk email:info@middletonpress.co.uk

A-978 0 906520 B- 978 1 873793 C- 978 1 901706 D-978 1 904474

E - 978 1 906008 F - 978 1 908174 G - 978 1 910356

All titles listed below were in print at time of publication - please check current availability by looking at our website - *www.middletonpress.co.uk* or by requesting a Brochure which includes our *LATEST* RAILWAY TITLES also our TRAMWAY, TROLLEYBUS, MILITARY and COASTAL series

A

Abergavenny to Merthyr C 91 8
Abertillery & Ebbw Vale Lines D 84 5
Aberystwyth to Carmarthen E 90 1
Allhallows - Branch Line to A 62 8
Alton - Branch Lines to A 11 6
Andover to Southampton A 82 6
Ascot - Branch Lines around A 64 2
Ashburton - Branch Line to B 95 4
Ashford - Steam to Eurostar B 67 1
Ashford to Dover A 48 2
Austrian Narrow Gauge D 04 3
Avonmouth - BL around D 42 5
Aylesbury to Rugby D 91 3

B

Baker Street to Uxbridge D 90 6
Bala to Llandudno E 87 1
Banbury to Birmingham D 27 2
Banbury to Cheltenham E 63 5
Bangor to Holyhead F 01 7
Bangor to Portmadoc E 72 7
Barking to Southend C 80 2
Barmouth to Pwllheli E 53 6
Barry - Branch Lines around D 50 0
Bartlow - Branch Lines to F 27 7
Bath Green Park to Bristol C 36 9
Bath to Evercreech Junction A 60 4
Beamish 40 years on rails E94 9
Bedford to Wellingborough D 31 9
Berwick to Drem F 64 2
Berwick to St. Boswells F 75 8
B'ham to Tamworth & Nuneaton F 63 5
Birkenhead to West Kirby F 61 1
Birmingham to Wolverhampton E253
Blackburn to Hellifield F 95 6
Bletchley to Cambridge D 94 4
Bletchley to Rugby E 07 9
Bodmin - Branch Lines around B 83 1
Boston to Lincoln F 80 2
Bournemouth to Evercreech Jn A 46 8
Bournemouth to Weymouth A 57 4
Bradshaw's History F18 5
Bradshaw's Rail Times 1850 F 13 0
Bradshaw's Rail Times 1895 F 11 6
Branch Lines series - see town names
Brecon to Neath D 43 2
Brecon to Newport D 16 6
Brecon to Newtown E 06 2
Brighton to Eastbourne A 16 1
Brighton to Worthing A 03 1
Bristol to Taunton D 03 6
Bromley South to Rochester B 23 7
Bromsgrove to Birmingham D 87 6
Bromsgrove to Gloucester D 73 9
Broxbourne to Cambridge F16 1
Brunel - A railtour D 74 6
Bude - Branch Line to B 29 9
Burnham to Evercreech Jn B 68 0

C

Cambridge to Ely D 55 5
Canterbury - BLs around B 58 9
Cardiff to Dowlais (Cae Harris) E 47 5
Cardiff to Pontypridd E 95 6
Cardiff to Swansea E 42 0
Carlisle to Hawick E 85 7
Carmarthen to Fishguard E 66 6
Caterham & Tattenham Corner B251
Central & Southern Spain NG E 91 8
Chard and Yeovil - BLs a C 30 7
Charing Cross to Dartford A 75 8
Charing Cross to Orpington A 96 3
Cheddar - Branch Line to B 90 9
Cheltenham to Andover C 43 7
Cheltenham to Redditch D 81 4
Chester to Birkenhead F 21 5
Chester to Manchester F 51 2
Chester to Rhyl E 93 2
Chester to Warrington F 40 6
Chichester to Portsmouth A 14 7
Clacton and Walton - BLs to F 04 8
Clapham Jn to Beckenham Jn B 36 7
Cleobury Mortimer - BLs a E 18 5
Clevedon & Portishead - BLs to D180
Consett to South Shields E 57 4
Cornwall Narrow Gauge D 56 2
Corris and Vale of Rheidol E 65 9
Coventry to Leicester G 00 5
Craven Arms to Llandeilo E 35 2
Craven Arms to Wellington E 33 8
Crawley to Littlehampton A 34 5
Crewe to Manchester F 57 4
Cromer - Branch Lines around C 26 0
Croydon to East Grinstead B 48 0
Crystal Palace & Catford Loop B 87 1
Cyprus Narrow Gauge E 13 0

D

Darjeeling Revisited F 09 3
Darlington Leamside Newcastle E 28 4
Darlington to Newcastle D 98 2
Dartford to Sittingbourne B 34 3
Denbigh - Branch Lines around F 32 1
Derby to Stoke-on-Trent F 93 2
Derwent Valley - BL to the D 06 7
Devon Narrow Gauge E 09 3
Didcot to Banbury D 02 9
Didcot to Swindon C 84 0
Didcot to Winchester C 13 0
Dorset & Somerset NG D 76 0
Douglas - Laxey - Ramsey E 75 8
Douglas to Peel C 88 8
Douglas to Port Erin C 55 0
Douglas to Ramsey D 39 5
Dover to Ramsgate A 78 9
Drem to Edinburgh G 06 7
Dublin Northwards in 1950s E 31 4
Dunstable - Branch Lines to E 27 7

E

Ealing to Slough C 42 0
Eastbourne to Hastings A 27 7
East Cornwall Mineral Railways D 22 7
East Croydon to Three Bridges A 53 6
Eastern Spain Narrow Gauge E 56 7
East Grinstead - BLs to A 07 9
East Kent Light Railway A 61 1
East London - Branch Lines of C 44 4
East London Line B 80 0
East of Norwich - Branch Lines E 69 7
Effingham Junction - BLs a A 74 1
Ely to Norwich C 90 1
Enfield Town & Palace Gates D 32 6
Epsom to Horsham A 30 7
Eritrean Narrow Gauge E 38 3
Euston to Harrow & Wealdstone C 89 5
Exeter to Barnstaple B 15 2
Exeter to Newton Abbot C 49 9
Exeter to Tavistock B 69 5
Exmouth - Branch Lines to B 00 8

F

Fairford - Branch Line to A 52 9
Falmouth, Helston & St. Ives C 74 1
Fareham to Salisbury A 67 3
Faversham to Dover B 05 3
Felixstowe & Aldeburgh - BL to D 20 3
Fenchurch Street to Barking C 20 8
Festiniog - 50 yrs of enterprise C 83 3
Festiniog 1946-55 E 01 7
Festiniog in the Fifties B 68 8
Festiniog in the Sixties B 91 6
Ffestiniog in Colour 1955-82 F 25 3
Finsbury Park to Alexandra Pal C 02 8
French Metre Gauge Survivors F 88 8
Frome to Bristol B 77 0

G

Galashiels to Edinburgh F 52 9
Gloucester to Bristol D 35 7
Gloucester to Cardiff D 66 1
Gosport - Branch Lines around A 36 9
Greece Narrow Gauge D 72 2

H

Hampshire Narrow Gauge D 36 4
Harrow to Watford D 14 2
Harwich & Hadleigh - BLs to F 02 4
Harz Revisited F 62 8
Hastings to Ashford A 37 6
Hawick to Galashiels F 36 9
Hawkhurst - Branch Line to A 66 6
Hayling - Branch Line to A 12 3
Hay-on-Wye - BL around D 92 0
Haywards Heath to Seaford A 28 4
Hemel Hempstead - BLs to D 88 3
Henley, Windsor & Marlow - BLa C77 2
Hereford to Newport D 54 8
Hertford & Hatfield - BLs a E 58 1
Hertford Loop E 71 0
Hexham to Carlisle D 75 3
Hexham to Hawick F 08 6
Hitchin to Peterborough D 07 4
Holborn Viaduct to Lewisham A 81 9
Horsham - Branch Lines to A 02 4
Huntingdon - Branch Line to A 93 2

I

Ilford to Shenfield C 97 0
Ilfracombe - Branch Line to B 21 3
Industrial Rlys of the South East A 09 3
Ipswich to Diss F 81 9
Ipswich to Saxmundham C 41 3
Isle of Man Railway Journey G 02 9
Isle of Wight Lines - 50 yrs C 12 3
Italy Narrow Gauge F 17 8

K

Kent Narrow Gauge C 45 1
Kettering to Nottingham F 82-6
Kidderminster to Shrewsbury E 10 9
Kingsbridge - Branch Line to C 98 7
Kings Cross to Potters Bar E 62 8
King's Lynn to Hunstanton F 58 1
Kingston & Hounslow Loops A 83 3
Kingswear - Branch Line to C 17 8

L

Lambourn - Branch Line to C 70 3
Launceston & Princetown - BLs C 19 2
Leek - Branch Line From G 01 2
Leicester to Burton F 85 7
Lewisham to Dartford A 92 5
Lincoln to Cleethorpes F 56 7
Lincoln to Doncaster G 03 6
Lines around Stamford F 98 7
Lines around Wimbledon B 75 6
Liverpool Street to Chingford D 01 2
Liverpool Street to Ilford C 34 5
Llandeilo to Swansea E 46 8
London Bridge to Addiscombe B 20 6
London Bridge to East Croydon A 58 1
Longmoor - Branch Lines to A 41 3
Looe - Branch Line to C 22 2
Loughborough to Nottingham F 68 0
Lowestoft - BLs around E 40 6
Ludlow to Hereford E 14 7
Lydney - Branch Lines around E 26 0
Lyme Regis - Branch Line to A 45 1
Lynton - Branch Line to B 04 6

M

Machynlleth to Barmouth E 54 3
Maesteg and Tondu Lines E 06 2
Majorca & Corsica Narrow Gauge F 41 3
March - Branch Lines around B 09 1
Market Drayton - BLs around F 67 3
Market Harborough to Newark F 86 4
Marylebone to Rickmansworth D 49 4
Melton Constable to Yarmouth Bch E031
Midhurst - Branch Lines of E 78 9
Midhurst - Branch Lines to F 00 0
Minehead - Branch Line to A 80 2
Mitcham Junction Lines B 01 5
Monmouth - Branch Lines to E 20 8
Monmouthshire Eastern Valleys D 71 5
Moretonhampstead - BL to C 27 7
Moreton-in-Marsh to Worcester D 26 5
Morpeth to Bellingham F 87 1
Mountain Ash to Neath D 80 7

N

Newark to Doncaster F 78 9
Newbury to Westbury C 66 6
Newcastle to Hexham D 69 2
Newport (IOW) - Branch Lines to A 26 0
Newquay - Branch Lines to C 71 0
Newton Abbot to Plymouth C 60 4
Newtown to Aberystwyth E 41 3
Northampton to Peterborough F 92 5
North East German NG D 44 9
Northern Alpine Narrow Gauge F 37 6
Northern France Narrow Gauge C 75 8
Northern Spain Narrow Gauge E 83 3
North London Line B 94 7
North of Birmingham F 55 0
North Woolwich - BLs around C 65 9
Nottingham to Boston F 70 3
Nottingham to Lincoln F 43 7

O

Ongar - Branch Line to E 05 5
Orpington to Tonbridge B 03 9
Oswestry - Branch Lines around E 60 4
Oswestry to Whitchurch E 81 9
Oxford to Bletchley D 57 9
Oxford to Moreton-in-Marsh D 15 9

P

Paddington to Ealing C 37 6
Paddington to Princes Risborough C819
Padstow - Branch Line to B 54 1
Pembroke and Cardigan - BLs to F 29 1
Peterborough to Kings Lynn E 32 1
Peterborough to Lincoln F 89 5
Peterborough to Newark F 72 7
Plymouth - BLs around B 98 5
Plymouth to St. Austell C 63 5
Pontypool to Mountain Ash D 65 4
Pontypridd to Merthyr F 14 7
Pontypridd to Port Talbot E 86 4
Porthmadog 1954-94 - BLa B 31 2
Portmadoc 1923-46 - BLa B 13 8
Portsmouth to Southampton A 31 4
Portugal Narrow Gauge E 67 3
Potters Bar to Cambridge D 70 8
Princes Risborough - BL to D 05 0
Princes Risborough to Banbury C 85 7

R

Railways to Victory C 16 1
Reading to Basingstoke B 27 5
Reading to Didcot C 79 6
Reading to Guildford A 47 5
Redhill to Ashford A 73 4
Return to Blaenau 1970-82 C 64 2
Rhyl to Bangor F 15 4
Rhymney & New Tredegar Lines E 48 2
Rickmansworth to Aylesbury D 61 6
Romania & Bulgaria NG E 23 9
Romneyrail C 32 1
Ross-on-Wye - BLs around E 30 7
Ruabon to Barmouth E 84 0
Rugby to Birmingham E 37 6
Rugby to Loughborough F 12 3
Rugby to Stafford F 07 9
Rugeley to Stoke-on-Trent F 90 1
Ryde to Ventnor A 19 2

S

Salisbury to Westbury B 39 8
Sardinia and Sicily Narrow Gauge F 50 5
Saxmundham to Yarmouth C 69 7
Saxony & Baltic Germany Revisited F 71 0
Saxony Narrow Gauge D 47 0
Seaton & Sidmouth - BLs to A 95 6
Selsey - Branch Line to A 04 8
Sheerness - Branch Line to B 16 2
Shenfield to Ipswich E 96 3
Shrewsbury - Branch Line to A 86 4
Shrewsbury to Chester E 70 3
Shrewsbury to Crewe F 48 2
Shrewsbury to Ludlow E 21 5
Shrewsbury to Newtown E 29 1
Sierra Leone Narrow Gauge D 28 9
Sirhowy Valley Line E 12 3
Sittingbourne to Ramsgate A 90 1
Skegness & Mablethorpe - BL to F 84 0
Slough to Newbury C 56 7
South African Two-foot gauge E 51 2
Southampton to Bournemouth A 42 0
Southend & Southminster BLs E 76 5
Southern Alpine Narrow Gauge F 22 2
Southern France Narrow Gauge C 47 5
South London Line B 46 6
South Lynn to Norwich City F 03 1
Southwold - Branch Line to A 15 4
Spalding - Branch Lines around E 52 9
Spalding to Grimsby F 65 9 6
Stafford to Chester F 34 5
Stafford to Wellington F 59 8
St Albans to Bedford D 08 1
St. Austell to Penzance C 67 3
St. Boswell to Berwick F 44 4
Steaming Through Isle of Wight A
Steaming Through West Hants A
Stourbridge to Wolverhampton E
St. Pancras to Barking D 68 5
St. Pancras to Folkestone E 88 8
St. Pancras to St. Albans C 78 9
Stratford to Cheshunt F 53 6
Stratford-u-Avon to Birmingham
Stratford-u-Avon to Cheltenham
Sudbury - Branch Lines to F 19 2
Surrey Narrow Gauge C 87 1
Sussex Narrow Gauge C 68 0
Swaffham - Branch Lines around
Swanage to 1999 - BL to A 33 8
Swanley to Ashford B 45 9
Swansea - Branch Lines around F
Swansea to Carmarthen E 59 8
Swindon to Bristol C 96 3
Swindon to Gloucester D 46 3
Swindon to Newport D 30 2
Swiss Narrow Gauge C 94 9

T

Talyllyn 60 E 98 7
Tamworth to Derby F 76 5
Taunton to Barnstaple B 60 2
Taunton to Exeter C 82 6
Taunton to Minehead F 39 0
Tavistock to Plymouth B 88 6
Tenterden - Branch Line to A 21 5
Three Bridges to Brighton A 35 2
Tilbury Loop C 86 4
Tiverton - BLs around C 62 8
Tivetshall to Beccles D 41 8
Tonbridge to Hastings A 44 4
Torrington - Branch Lines to B 37
Tourist Railways of France G 04 3
Towcester - BLs around E 39 0
Tunbridge Wells BLs A 32 1

U

Upwell - Branch Line to B 64 0
Uttoxeter to Macclesfield G 05 0

V

Victoria to Bromley South A 98 7
Victoria to East Croydon A 40 6
Vivarais Revisited E 08 6

W

Walsall Routes F 45 1
Wantage - Branch Line to D 25 8
Wareham to Swanage 50 yrs D098
Waterloo to Windsor A 54 3
Waterloo to Woking A 38 3
Watford to Leighton Buzzard D 45
Wellingborough to Leicester F 73 4
Welshpool to Llanfair E 49 9
Wenford Bridge to Fowey C 09 3
Westbury to Bath B 55 8
Westbury to Taunton C 76 5
West Cornwall Mineral Rlys D 48 7
West Croydon to Epsom B 08 4
West German Narrow Gauge D 93
West London - BLs of C 50 5
West London Line B 84 8
West Wiltshire - BLs of D 12 8
Weymouth - BLs A 65 9
Willesden Jn to Richmond B 71 8
Wimbledon to Beckenham C 58 1
Wimbledon to Epsom B 62 6
Wimborne - BLs around A 97 0
Wisbech - BLs around C 01 7
Witham & Kelvedon - BLs a E 82 6
Woking to Alton A 59 8
Woking to Portsmouth A 25 3
Woking to Southampton A 55 0
Wolverhampton to Shrewsbury E44
Wolverhampton to Stafford F 79 6
Worcester to Birmingham D 97 5
Worcester to Hereford D 38 8
Worthing to Chichester A 06 2
Wrexham to New Brighton F 47 5
Wroxham - BLs around F 31 4

Y

Yeovil - 50 yrs change C 38 3
Yeovil to Dorchester A 76 5
Yeovil to Exeter A 91 8
York to Scarborough F 23 9